The Price of Being Born

by

Thuli Marutle Leigh

The Price of Being Born
© 2025 by Thuli Marutle Leigh
All rights reserved.

No part of this publication may be reproduced, distributed, or transmitted in any form or by any means, including photocopying, recording, or other electronic or mechanical methods, without the prior written permission of the publisher, except in the case of brief quotations used in reviews and critical articles.

For permission requests, please contact:
Thuli Marutle Leigh
Email: mt.marutle@gmail.com

ISBN: 978-1-0492-1280-7 (ebook)
ISBN: 978-1-997482-02-4 (print)
First Edition — 2025

Independently Published

All characters, names, and situations are either used fictitiously or are meant for educational and reflective purposes. Any resemblance to real persons, living or dead, is purely coincidental.

DEDICATION

For the ones who gave everything and forgot themselves.

For every firstborn who carried too much too soon, every son and daughter who confused love with obligation, and every parent who will learn from Lebo's story that love should build, not break.

May this book remind us all — that love is not debt, and family is not a cage.

PREFACE

This is a story for every young person who has felt pressured to repay a life they never asked for. It isn't about rejecting family; it's about love without exploitation and the right to build your own future.

Too often, love is mistaken for obligation, and gratitude becomes a lifelong debt. But true love — the kind that nurtures rather than controls — gives without keeping score. It allows space for growth, individuality, and freedom.

This book invites reflection on the invisible expectations we inherit and the quiet power of choosing yourself — not out of selfishness, but out of self-respect. Because the greatest gift we can give back to those who raised us is to become whole, without losing ourselves in the process.

TABLE OF CONTENTS

Part I — Dreams and Beginnings
Chapter 1: A Child with Big Dreams
Chapter 2: First Paycheck
Chapter 3: The Never-Ending List

Part II — Cracks in the Foundation
Chapter 4: When Home Feels Heavy
Chapter 5: The Mansion Demand
Chapter 6: Dreams Crumble

Part III — The Price Unfolds
Chapter 7: Alone with Debt
Chapter 8: The Dinner
Chapter 9: The Breaking Point

Part IV — The Cost and the Consequence
Chapter 10: The Goodbye
Chapter 11: The Price of Being Born
Chapter 12: Aftermath

CHAPTER ONE
A CHILD WITH BIG DREAMS

Before they became parents, Sizwe and Tebatso dreamed boldly. They were young, in love, and brimming with ambition — she wanted a doctorate and a career in education, he dreamed of owning his own company and building a mansion that touched the sky. They planned late into the night, notebooks filled with sketches of degrees, houses, travel plans, and the good life they believed they could build.

Then, unexpectedly but joyfully, Tebatso found out she was pregnant.

It was not part of the timeline. Marriage had been something they thought they would do later, after the degrees, after a few more pay raises. But when they saw the tiny heartbeat on the scan, everything changed. They chose each other fully and got married so their baby would be born into a secure home. They were nervous, yes, but overwhelmed with love. In their hearts, this child became their new dream.

They named him Lebo.

From the start, they built their lives around him. Careers were adjusted, savings rerouted, and the adventurous futures they had imagined were quietly placed on hold. Sizwe took on work that paid the bills but didn't feed his soul. Tebatso traded postgraduate ambitions for tutoring and extra jobs that kept the household running. They told themselves it was worth it because Lebo would have the perfect childhood.

And he did.

Lebo grew up surrounded by warmth — bedtime stories, Saturday pancakes, parents cheering at every award. He wore crisp school uniforms while his friends wore hand-me-downs. He attended good private schools and extra lessons his parents could barely afford. If he needed something for school, they found a way. He was their pride, their investment, their proof that love meant giving everything.

They never complained. But their sacrifices were gently spoken out loud — reminders wrapped in love.

"One day, you'll thank us, my boy," his father would say with a proud smile.

"We've put our dreams on hold so you can chase yours," his mother would add, half joking, half praying it would pay off.

A Growing Family

For a long time, it was just the three of them — a tight little unit with Lebo at the center. But life had more surprises.

When Lebo was finishing primary school and just about to start high school, Tebatso found out she was pregnant again. At first there was shock; the family's finances were already stretched thin. But joy won out. Soon baby Khomotso arrived — a soft little sister whom Lebo adored. He was old enough to help, and the house filled with baby giggles and diapers once more.

A few years later, just as Lebo was preparing for his last years of high school, Tebatso discovered she was pregnant again — this time with twins. After a complicated but safe pregnancy, Thabang and Nthati were born. Two more little lives. Two more reasons Sizwe and Tebatso worked late and sacrificed more.

Lebo loved his siblings deeply. He was proud to be the big brother. But with each new baby came new weight on his young shoulders. Everyone said it openly:

"You're the firstborn, Lebo. You'll take care of your brother and sisters one day."

"Big brothers are the foundation of the family."

"Your parents have done everything for you; when you succeed, you'll help them raise the others."

It was said with smiles, sometimes laughter. But it was also serious. Lebo learned early that success was not just about himself — it was about everyone who depended on him.

He was a naturally bright child, curious and determined. Teachers praised him: gifted, promising, destined for great things. His parents beamed with pride at every report card. Church elders prayed over him: "May this boy lift his family." Neighbors told him, "You will change their lives."

Lebo liked the sound of it. He dreamed of being a doctor, an engineer, maybe an entrepreneur. He wanted to be the one who finally gave his parents the life they had once dreamed of but gave up for him. He wanted to send his siblings to the best schools, buy his mom the big kitchen she wanted, give his dad the rest he deserved.

He didn't know that wanting to help and being expected to help would one day feel like two very different things.

Dreams And Pride

He was a naturally bright child, curious and determined.

Teachers praised him: gifted, promising, destined for great things. His parents beamed with pride at every report card. Church elders prayed over him:

"May this boy lift his family." Neighbors told him,

"You will change their lives."

Lebo liked the sound of it. He dreamed of being a doctor, an engineer, maybe an entrepreneur. He wanted to be the one who finally gave his parents the life they had once dreamed of but gave up for him. He wanted to send his siblings to the best schools, buy his mom the big kitchen she wanted, give his dad the rest he deserved.

He didn't know that wanting to help and being expected to help would one day feel like two very different things.

Quiet Moments of Pressure

Sometimes, late at night, he overheard his parents worrying about bills.

Sizwe would rub his face tiredly and sigh, "It's okay. One day, Lebo will soon finish school and help take care of us."

Tebatso would nod, then go back to tutoring long hours to pay school fees.

At birthday parties or family gatherings, uncles and aunts would grin and say:

"This one is our future. Don't forget us when you're grown and rich!"

It was love, but it was also a seed planted deep — a seed that said: You owe us for existing.

A Promise Made in Innocence

One night after a school awards ceremony, Lebo - now a tall, proud teenager - came home clutching a trophy for academic excellence. His parents were glowing. Over dinner he said, half-joking but wholly sincere:

"One day, I'll buy you the biggest house and make sure Khomotso, Thabang, and Nthati have everything they need."

The room erupted in joy. Sizwe clapped him on the back. Tebatso's eyes welled up. The younger children giggled, imagining a future with their big brother as a hero.

Lebo felt proud and strong. He didn't know that the promise he had just made would one day feel like a contract signed in invisible ink.

Foreshadowing the Price

That night, he went to bed with big dreams.
He thought success was simple: study hard, get a great job, take care of the people who took care of him.

He didn't yet know how heavy that dream could become - or how love, when mixed with obligation, can turn into a debt you never asked for.

CHAPTER TWO
FIRST PAYCHEQUE

Lebo's first real job felt like stepping into sunlight after years of study.

He had worked hard - long nights in lecture halls, tutoring other students to stretch his bursary, taking every opportunity he could find. At last, a respected engineering firm in Johannesburg offered him a junior position.

When the offer letter arrived, his parents threw a small celebration: neighbours came over, cousins cheered, and Sizwe made a speech about hard work paying off.

"Our boy is a man now!" his father said, pride radiating like heat.

"We gave him roots; now he will fly," Tebatso added with tears in her eyes.

For Lebo, the first day at the office felt like a dream: new shirt, fresh tie, polished shoes he'd saved for. After work he messaged his mom: "I made it. First day done." She replied with hearts and prayers.

When the first paycheck hit his account a month later, Lebo stared at the numbers in disbelief. It wasn't huge, but to him it was gold - proof he could stand on his own. For a moment, he imagined what he might do: buy the phone he'd wanted, upgrade his laptop, maybe start saving for a small car.

But the messages came quickly - and lovingly.

Mama: "My boy, can you help with Khomotso's school shoes? She's outgrown the old ones."

Papa: "We're short on the twins' school fees this month. Just until we catch up."

Auntie Lindiwe: "Your uncle is sick; we're collecting for his medicine."

It didn't feel like a burden - not yet. It felt right.
Lebo smiled as he transferred almost everything away.

They gave me everything, he thought. They worked so hard so I could be here. Of course they deserve this first salary. Next month I'll start saving for me.

A Friend's Freedom

A few days later, Lebo's phone buzzed with a call from Tebello, his old varsity friend.

"Bro! Guess what? I'm buying my first car today.
Come with me!"

Lebo blinked. A car?
He hadn't expected that. Your first paycheque? he thought. Already?

Still, he laughed and agreed. "Of course! Let's go."

When they met at the dealership, Tebello was buzzing — wide smile, keys already in hand for a test drive. The car gleamed under the showroom lights.

On the ride, Lebo finally asked the question swirling in his head.

"Hey, Tebza... so, your first salary — didn't your parents need help? School stuff? Bills? You're really just buying a car?"

Tebello chuckled.

"Of course I gave them something. A small thank-you. But they told me to keep most of it — to enjoy myself. My dad said, 'You've worked hard, make yourself happy. Start your life.' So... I did."

Lebo smiled, nodded, pretended he wasn't surprised.

Inside, a thought stirred: Imagine having that kind of freedom.

But it didn't cut deep — not yet.

He told himself: This is just my first salary. My parents sacrificed everything. They deserve this one. Next month, I'll start saving for my car. I don't want debt anyway. And sooner rather than later I would love to move out of my parent's house and be a grown up.

Out loud he said:
"I'm saving to buy mine cash. Don't want any debts and risk missing payments and my name being blacklisted."

Tebello slapped his shoulder.
"Smart move, bro! Wish I had your discipline."
Lebo smiled. It felt good to be praised, even if the reason for his "discipline" was simply that there was nothing left to spend.

First Sacrifices

That night, Lebo checked his account - nearly empty after helping with school fees, groceries, and medicine. He shrugged it off. His heart was light. They needed me. I came through.

He postponed the phone upgrade and told himself the laptop could wait. As for the car — it would happen and it's probably best to save up and buy it cash. He'd save. Next month would be different.

Around him, family members sent grateful messages:

"God bless you, my son."

"We're proud of you, Lebo."

"You're a good brother."

The words felt warm. He slept smiling.

Ayanda

Around this time, Lebo met Ayanda at a mutual friend's gathering - smart, kind, with an easy laugh. She was drawn to his humility; he was charmed by her calm confidence. On their first few dates, she admired how he spoke of his family.

"You really take care of them," she said once, touched.

He grinned, a little shy.
"They've done so much for me. It's only right."

She smiled but looked thoughtful, as if filing the detail away. She didn't say much — not yet.

Hopeful Plans

By the end of that first working month, Lebo still felt optimistic. Yes, he had given almost everything away, but it was only the beginning. He told himself his parents would stabilize soon, the requests would slow, and he'd start building his own life.

He didn't know that the second paycheck - and the ones after it - would disappear just as fast, for now, he believed in the promise he'd made long ago at that dinner table: to take care of the family who had given him everything. He believed he could do that and still build his own future.

He didn't yet know how quickly that hope would be tested.

CHAPTER THREE
THE NEVER-ENDING LIST

Lebo thought he understood what helping his family would look like.

When he landed the job, he told himself: I'll send groceries home every month and chip in if something big comes up. The rest I'll save for me — a car, a small place of my own, maybe a holiday one day.
It felt fair.

The first month disappeared faster than he expected, but he told himself it was just because it was the first: extra textbooks for Khomotso, school fees, exam fees, a sick uncle's medication.
"Next month will be mine," he whispered.

Another Payday, Another List

The second payday arrived. Lebo smiled at the number in his account; his probation at work was finally over, so this month's salary was a bit more. Already planning to finally start a savings pot, he exhaled in relief.

Then the messages arrived.

Papa: "My boy, Khomotso's school wants another textbook this term, and the twins' fees are short again. Can you help before they send a final notice?"

Mama: "Lebo, the kitchen tiles are falling apart.
We've been patching them for years. Maybe this month, if you can, we could start fixing the ones by the sink."

Auntie Lindiwe: "There's a funeral this weekend.
Every household must make a contribution "

Each message was reasonable by itself. Together, they were almost his whole pay. Again. He stared at the screen, the quiet ache of disappointment tapping at his chest. He shoved it aside. They've done so much for me. It's my turn now. Next month will be mine.

He transferred the money, filled a grocery cart for home, watched his balance fall like daylight in winter.

Ayanda Gives Instead of Taking

A few weeks later, Ayanda called.
"I'm stealing you for dinner tomorrow," she teased.

They met at a warm little restaurant with candles flickering low. They laughed, shared memories, let the world fall away. For two hours he wasn't a provider, just a man on a date. When the bill came, he reached for his wallet out of habit.

"Lebo, don't worry," Ayanda said, laying her hand gently over his. "I planned this ahead and paid when I booked the table."

He blinked. "Are you sure? Let me send you the money."

She smiled, gentle but firm.
"No. Let me do this. You do so much for everyone.
Tonight is on me."

Something inside him shifted. He wasn't used to receiving with no strings attached. He swallowed a lump in his throat and simply said, "Thank you."

The next day, he spent almost the last of what remained in his account on a small bouquet of flowers. He slipped a note between the stems:

Thanks for dinner... everyone just takes and you gave. I'll never forget this. I promise to make it up to you - you're on my mind.

Ayanda smiled when she found the flowers waiting that day at work. She read the words twice, her smile softening into warmth. It wasn't flashy, but it felt deeply thoughtful - the kind of gesture that says I see you, and 1 appreciate you.
She felt loved and quietly proud of the man she was getting to know.Lebo had made her day.

Ayanda's Birthday

A month later it was Ayanda's birthday.
Lebo had planned to do something special, but the month's "little things" had eaten everything again: more school fees, a funeral contribution, and the start of the kitchen tiles Mama had longed for. By the time her birthday arrived, his account was almost empty.

He sent a warm but simple text: Happy birthday, beautiful. Wishing you the best year yet.

She replied politely and thanked him, but the joy she'd felt when she saw the flowers weeks earlier dulled. She had hoped for more — a dinner, a small thoughtful gift, even just effort.

Quietly, she pulled back.

Calls became short, texts less frequent. She didn't say why; she just felt a little unseen. At some point he thought maybe Lebo had planned some surprise for her until her birthday passed and she realised that wasn't the case.

Tebello's Call From the Airport

Not long after, Tebello called, his voice full of sunshine.

"Bro! Do me a favour? I'm flying to Mauritius this afternoon for a week. Can you drop me at the airport? Keep my car while I'm gone - drive it, stretch its legs. Just fetch me next Sunday."

Lebo laughed, surprised and touched. "Are you serious?"

"Absolutely. You've been grinding nonstop. Enjoy a comfortable ride for once."

He took Tebello to the airport, hugged him goodbye, and drove back alone. The car was smooth and quiet, the engine a gentle hum. Air-con crisp, music soft, seats that felt like they belonged to someone free. For the first time in months, he felt... light.

I wish this was mine, he thought. Just the freedom to drive where I want, when I want.

The Driveway Interrogation

When he pulled into the family yard, Mama came out wiping her hands with a dish cloth, Papa close behind. Their faces were surprise edged with worry.

"Lebo," Papa said carefully, "how will you pay for this car with school fees and everything else? We are still catching up."

"And the tiles," Mama added, hand on her hip. "We haven't finished the kitchen."

Lebo laughed, hands raised swiftly as if the police had shouted an instruction. "Relax, relax - it's not mine. Tebello's on vacation. I dropped him at the airport; he said I can keep it for a week and fetch him Sunday."

The relief was instant.

"Eish, okay," Papa exhaled, chuckling. "I was worried - thinking how will our boy manage this and still help us?"

"Aowa, at least it's not that," Mama said, stroking the bonnet like a guest. "It's beautiful though.
One day, you'll have your own."

"One day," Lebo echoed with a smile that didn't reach his chest.

Driving later that night, the leather steering wheel warm under his hands, the truth landed softly but firmly: A car may not happen for me soon. My salary is already spoken for before I even touch it.

A week later Tebello calls asking Lebo to continue keeping the car because he wasn't coming back anytime soon, he had asked for more days at work and wanted to stay there a bit longer. Lebo was happy but at the same time he didn't want to get used to something that wasn't his.

Lebo's Birthday

Weeks later it was Lebo's birthday. His parents threw a small, homely celebration - cake from the corner bakery, a pot of beef stew on the stove, some chakalaka, coleslaw salad and pap with neighbours and siblings crowding the lounge.

Ayanda decided to come, even though her heart was still a little sore from her own birthday. She smiled, greeted everyone warmly, watched from the couch as the day unfolded.

She saw what Lebo had never really described: every time something was short, a head turned to him.

"We're out of salt - Lebo, can you run to the shop?"

"Your aunt's stuck; send her taxi money."

"Khomo needs data for her homework."

He reached for his wallet or his phone each time, quietly, naturally, as if this was simply air and gravity. Nobody else moved to help. Nobody even looked ashamed.

After dinner plates were cleared and the living room filled with chatter, Lebo stepped out to the back step for a moment of quiet. Ayanda noticed and followed him. He looked tired but still warm, smiling faintly from the day.

"Lebo," she said softly, "how do you cope?"

He hesitated, then shrugged, trying for casual but not quite making it.

"I just… do. They need me. I'm the eldest. It's what's expected."

She touched his arm.

"You give so much. Don't you ever keep anything for yourself?"

He stared at the dark street, finally allowing the words he'd held in for years.

"I thought I'd just help with groceries. But every month there's something — school fees, tiles, funerals, taxi fare. It's never enough, but I can't say no. They gave up so much for me… how do I not give back?"

She listened quietly, no judgment, only care.

"I don't want you to drown," she said.

He gave a small, grateful smile. For a long moment, they sat together. Then she leaned in and kissed him — gentle, unexpected, but certain.

When they pulled apart, they were shy but smiling, something unspoken settling between them.

A voice called from inside, bright and happy:

"Cake time!"

They both laughed quietly and went back in, side by side.

Cake and the Watch

Everyone crowded around as the candles were lit and a birthday song filled the room. Before he could blow out the candles, Ayanda placed a small box in front of him.

"For you," she said simply.

Lebo opened it - a sleek, handsome watch. His eyes widened; he hadn't expected anything and feeling ashamed because he couldn't get her anything for her birthday.

"Ayanda.. wow. Thank you."

The room fell briefly quiet. His parents smiled politely but seemed unsure. One of the relatives half-joked to break the silence:

"Well, we gave him an education. That's a gift too."

A few people laughed lightly, but the moment felt thin. Ayanda just smiled at Lebo, who met her gaze with gratitude and a touch of sadness.

Quiet Realisation

That night, after everyone left and the house quieted, Lebo sat with the watch on his wrist. It felt like more than time - it felt like someone finally seeing him. He loved his family deeply, but he couldn't ignore the quiet truth forming inside: the list wasn't shrinking. It was learning the shape of his paydays and expanding to fill them.

He wasn't angry. Just tired. And aware for the first time that love, when it forgets balance, can quietly turn into debt.

He looked at the watch again and thought of Ayanda's soft voice: I don't want you to drown.

For the first time, he wondered if he might be starting to sink.

CHAPTER FOUR
WHEN HOME FEELS HEAVY

Lebo's room hadn't changed much since varsity. The same faded posters, the same study desk pressed under the window, the same small wardrobe fighting to hold too many shirts.

He'd once promised himself, as soon as I get a steady salary, I'll move out.
But months had become years, and that dream — like most of his - had quietly learned to wait its turn behind everyone else's needs.

The only new thing was the car outside -
Tebello's car — still parked neatly under the guava tree. Tebello had left it with him for more than a month now before flying to Mauritius. "Keep it for me, bro. Stretch its legs." At first Lebo thought he'd fetch it in a week or two. He never did. Now it sat gleaming quietly, like a guest overstaying its welcome, reminding everyone that it wasn't his. Neighbours sometimes waved when they saw him drive it to the shop.

"Our Lebo's doing well!" they'd say.

He'd smile and wave back, never correcting them. It was easier to let them believe the picture - the car, the good job, the nice clothes - than to explain the truth:
Everything that looks like mine belongs to someone else.

A Full House, an Empty Heart

The house was always busy.
Mama's voice calling from the kitchen, pots clattering on the stove.

Papa on the phone, giving advice to some cousin.

Children running through the passage, laughter echoing down the hall.
From the outside, it looked like joy.

But the fuller the house became, the lonelier Lebo felt.

Every month he tried again to save for his own place. Every month, the list arrived first - like rent he paid for being born.
He didn't mind helping; it was the unspoken rule of eldest sons. But lately, it felt less like helping and more like being harvested.

Ayanda's Visit

Ayanda came by one Saturday afternoon, smiling like she always did.
She brought food she'd cooked herself - rice and a whole seven colors with fried chicken that almost looked like kentucky, and a black forest cake that made the whole house smell like peace.

Mama welcomed her politely, Papa nodded, the siblings peeked shyly from behind doors.
After lunch, she and Lebo sat under the guava tree where the plastic chairs leaned toward each other like tired friends.

"You still haven't moved out?" she asked gently.

He smiled, a little embarrassed. "You sound like me a year ago."

"So what's stopping you?"

He exhaled. "Rent, furniture, deposit — all those adult things.
I'll get there."

Ayanda tilted her head. "Lebo... when will you get there? Every time I ask, it's 'after this, 'after that! You're always waiting for everyone else's life to settle before you start living yours." He didn't answer. He just stared at the ground, picking at the dust with his shoe.

She leaned closer. "You take care of everyone. Who's taking care of you?"

He smiled faintly, but it never reached his eyes.

Family Conversations

That evening, as the sun dipped low, Mama called from the kitchen.

"Lebo, don't forget the stovel payment is due on Monday, neh? You said you'd help again."

He nodded automatically. "Yes, Mama."

A few minutes later, Papa joined in. "And we must start planning the extension soon. The girls are getting big, they need space."

Lebo rubbed his temples. "Papa, can we maybe wait a bit? I'm trying to save."

Papa frowned, disappointment already softening his tone. "We just thought... with your good job-"

"I know," Lebo interrupted gently. "Just... not now."

Papa said nothing more, but the silence that followed said everything.

Restless Night

Later that night, the house had finally quieted - the TV off, the dishes done, everyone asleep.

Lebo sat by the window, watching Tebello's car glint faintly under the porch light.
He could drive it anytime, but lately he hadn't touched it.It reminded him too much of the freedom that didn't belong to him.

Just then he decided to call Tebello, but he didn't answer.Instead he sent a text:

"What's up bro,where I am is so noisy. Don't worry I'm all good,I'm clubbing right now.I won't be coming back anytime soon, my boss agreed for me to work online.I will give you a call tomorrow"!

He unlocked his phone once more and read Tebello's text and scrolled past the bank messages he didn't want to read.A new one blinked at the top - Ayanda:Don't forget your own dreams, Lebo. Please.

He smiled softly, typing back:One day.

But even as he sent it, he knew the truth - One day was beginning to sound a lot like never.

CHAPTER FIVE
THE MANSION DEMAND

Tebello's message came early one bright Saturdaymorning:"Bro, I'm back in Joburg! Finally coming to get the car. Hope you didn't sell it!"

Lebo smiled faintly. The car had been both pride and pain - a symbol of freedom that wasn't truly his. Maybe it was time to let it go.

A Visit from Tebello
By afternoon, Tebello's familiar laugh rolled into the yard.They hugged, catching up between jokes and back slaps.

"Haibo, Lebza!" he exclaimed, patting the bonnet."You've looked after her like a baby. You even waxed it!"

Lebo chuckled. "You don't know half the drama this car caused."

Tebello raised an eyebrow. "What drama?"

Lebo grinned, shaking his head. "The first day I brought it home, my parents almost had a heart attack."

Tebello laughed. "A heart attack? Why?"

"They thought it was mine!"
He mimicked his mother's voice. "Lebo, the tiles? We haven't finished the kitchen."

Then his father's: "How will you pay for this car with school fees?"

Tebello bent over, laughing. "Yoh! Did they really say that?"

"I had to explain it's your car. The relief on their faces.." Lebo shook his head, half smiling. "They were so proud it wasn't mine." The laughter softened into silence.

The Truth Comes Out

Tebello's tone shifted. "Why though? Shouldn't they be happy if it was yours?"

Lebo hesitated, his eyes on the dusty ground. "Because they think anything I buy for myself takes something from them. Every month it's a new list - school fees, funerals, repairs. I can't say no. If I ever keep something for myself, the guilt eats me alive."

Tebello leaned back against the car, quiet for a moment. "So you're basically paying to exist?"

Lebo exhaled, his smile fading. "That's one way to put it."

Drinks and Confessions

After a long pause, Tebello stood up. "Come, we're not having this talk in the yard. Let's go somewhere — nearest Chesa Nyama, my treat. We need a drink and some meat."

They drove to a small place by the roadside, ordered beers while someone was preparing their meat and settled into a booth. The music was soft since it was a Sunday, the kind that made people think deep and talk honestly.

After a few sips, Lebo loosened up. "You know, I've never really told anyone this stuff."

"That's what I'm here for," Tebello said. "Talk."

Lebo nodded slowly. "I've been helping my family since my first paycheck. I thought it would get easier. But now it's just expected. I can't move out, can't save, can't breathe."

Tebello frowned. "And you've never told them you need space?"

"I tried once," Lebo said, voice low. "They said, 'We raised you, fed you, educated you - now you want to abandon us?'"

He took another drink, the bitterness mixing with guilt. After a moment, he smiled faintly.

"But I met someone. Ayanda."

Tebello looked up, surprised. "You? The secretive one?"

Lebo nodded, eyes softening. "She's special, Tebs. She doesn't take — she gives. One time she paid for our dinner without telling me. Just said,'You always do so much for everyone. Tonight's on me.'"
He smiled faintly. "I didn't even know how to react. I felt... seen." I couldn't even afford to get her anything for her birthday but she still stayed bro.

Tebello leaned forward, serious now. "Then you need to make room for her in your life. You can't build a home in your old bedroom. You need privacy, bro. Independence. Tell them it's time. Tell them you're not leaving them - you're just growing up." Before you lose this girl.

Lebo chuckled. "Easier said than done."

Tebello raised his glass. "You just don't have the strength yet. Drink. Maybe the courage is in here."

The Confrontation

By the time Tebello dropped him off, the night air was cool and heavy with crickets. Lebo wasn't drunk, but the edge of fear had dulled enough to make him brave.

He walked straight into the lounge, where Mama and Papa were watching TV.

"Mama. Papa. I need to talk."

They turned, surprised. His voice was steady, his eyes clear.

"I've been thinking... I want to move out. I'm older now. I have someone special, and I need my space. PIl still help, I'll still visit, but it's time l start my life."

For a moment, there was silence. Then Mama's face hardened.

"It's that girl, isn't it?"

"Mama, no-"

"I knew it!" she snapped. "I knew she was sly. She wants to break our home and take you for herself!"

Papa joined in, calmer but firm. "Lebo, we understand love. But this house runs because of you. You're the eldest. You know that."

He swallowed hard. "I'm not trying to abandon anyone. I just want-"

Mama cut him off, tears in her voice. "We sacrificed everything for you, and now you want to run away because of a woman?"

The room felt smaller with every word.
He looked between them, his courage slipping away as quickly as it came.
"I just thought you'd understand," he said quietly, before walking out to the yard.

The Beginning of the End

Under the guava tree, the one where Ayanda once brought lunch, he sat alone.
The night was quiet except for the distant hum of the city - the world moving on without him. He wanted to call Ayanda but didn't. What could he say? That he'd tried to choose himself and failed?

Inside, the TV laughter carried faintly through the walls. He closed his eyes and whispered:

"Maybe Tebello's right. I just don't have the strength yet."

He looked up at the house glowing softly under the moon - the house that loved him, needed him, and was slowly consuming him.

CHAPTER SIX
Dreams Crumble

Lebo moved out at the end of the month.

He packed his clothes, books, and the few things that were truly his into small boxes - nothing fancy, just quiet steps toward freedom.His parents watched, faces tight, offering help with their hands but not their hearts.Mama's smile didn't reach her eyes.
Papa's voice was calm, but his silence was heavy.

On the day he left, Mama hugged him a little too tightly and whispered,

"You'll see, that girl will be the reason this family breaks apart."

He didn't argue. He'd learned that sometimes silence was safer than truth.

Family Dinner

Lebo still came home for Sunday dinners.
At first, he brought Ayanda along, wanting to bridge the gap.But every visit felt like walking into a quiet storm.

Mama greeted Ayanda with polite smiles that froze at the corners.
Papa asked about her job, her family - the questions polite on the surface, sharp underneath.And every time Lebo said no to a request, eyes turned to her.

"He's changed since that girl came," Aunt Lindiwe would murmur.

"It's her," Mama would sigh later. "She's wants all my son's money to herself."

Ayanda, always calm, tried to explain kindly,
"He's paying rent now, Mama. He's trying to manage everything."
But her softness was mistaken for manipulation.

"You see?" Mama would whisper to Papa when they were alone. "She's clever with her tongue - she's making him forget us."
Lebo could feel the wall growing, one visit at a time.

A Step Toward Love

A few months later, Lebo made a decision.
He told his parents over dinner, voice gentle but sure.

"I've asked Ayanda to move in with me."

Forks froze midair.
Mama's eyes widened, Papa's jaw tightened. Mama spoke first.

"Move in? Without marriage?"

"It's temporary," Lebo said quickly. "We want to see how we live together. I love her."

Papa leaned back slowly. "That's fine," he said after a pause. "But don't think of getting married yet. Not until you've renovated this house."

Lebo blinked. "Papa, what?"
"You heard me," he said firmly. "This family had plans before marriage came into the picture. Finish what you started. Build this home properly first, then we'll bless your marriage."

Mama nodded. "Yes. Any woman who loves you will wait."

Lebo felt the old pressure return - the invisible chain tightening around his chest.
Ayanda sat quietly, her expression unreadable, but her fingers clenched under the table.

Different Worlds

A week later, Ayanda's family invited Lebo for lunch.

He went expecting the same tension, the same unspoken price tags.
Instead, he found warmth.

Ayanda's father met him at the gate with a handshake that turned into a hug.
Her mother insisted he sit down before even greeting properly.When he offered the drinks he'd bought, her mother smiled and said,

"No, no, my boy - never bring anything again.This is home. You're one of us."

He laughed awkwardly, unsure what to do with kindness that asked for nothing.
They ate, they talked, they laughed.
No one mentioned money. No one hinted at expectations.When he tried to help clean afterward, Ayanda's father waved him off.

"You're a guest today. Next time, maybe son-in-law. But still family either way."

Driving home that evening, Lebo stared out the window in silence. For the first time, he realized what family was supposed to feel like - love without a bill attached.

CHAPTER SEVEN
ALONE WITH DEBT

Weeks after Ayanda moved in, life found a new rhythm - quiet, simple, almost peaceful.
Lebo was learning to breathe again, though guilt still followed him like a shadow. He'd begun saying no sometimes - gently, carefully - and even that small word carried its own weight at home.

His parents tolerated it, but the coldness grew. He felt it in their silences, their glances, their sudden "we'll manage" responses.
And somehow, every bit of that unspoken tension found its way back to Ayanda.

A Call from Her Father

One afternoon, Lebo's phone rang - a number he didn't recognize.

"Good afternoon, Lebo. This is Mr. Dlamini - Ayanda's father."

Lebo straightened up immediately. "Good afternoon, sir! How are you?"

"I'm well, my boy. I was wondering if you'd have time for coffee tomorrow. Just us men. I'd like to talk about the future."

Lebo's throat tightened slightly. "Of course, sir. I'd be honoured."

"Good. Let's meet at that café near the taxi rank, 10 a.m.?"

"Yes, sir. I'll be there."

Man to Man

The next morning, they sat across from each other - the older man's calm presence commanding quiet respect.

Mr. Dlamini spoke first.

"Lebo, you're a good man. My wife and I can see you love our daughter and that she loves you. That's why I wanted to talk."

Lebo nodded, unsure where it was going.

"You know, I was raised in a different time. I understand the world has changed - people live together now, they test the waters before marriage. But I still believe in doing things the right way."

He paused, looking directly at Lebo.

"I won't lecture you. I just want to make sure your intentions are serious — that my daughter isn't just renting space in someone's life."

Lebo's chest tightened, but he met the man's gaze with honesty.
"Sir, I understand completely. I love Ayanda. I do want to marry her - I just... need to get my house in order first. Things have been a bit complicated lately, but I'm working toward it. It'll happen sooner than you think."

Mr. Dlamini smiled kindly.

"That's good to hear. Just remember, it's not about being rich or perfect - it's about being ready. My daughter deserves love, peace, and a home that doesn't feel like a battlefield."

Lebo nodded. "I promise you, sir. I'll make sure of that."

The News

When he got home that evening, Ayanda was sitting on the couch, her hands folded tightly in her lap. She looked nervous - pale, almost fragile.

He smiled gently. "You okay? You look like someone who's seen a ghost."

She tried to smile, but her eyes were full.
"I wasn't feeling well today," she said softly. "I threw up at work. My colleague forced me to see the doctor."

He frowned, stepping closer. "What did they say? Are you okay?"

Ayanda looked up, her voice barely a whisper. "Lebo... I'm pregnant."

For a moment, everything stopped.
The sound of the fridge, the faint hum of traffic outside - even his breathing.

Pregnant

She searched his face, her voice trembling.
"I found out this afternoon. I didn't know how to tell you."

He sank slowly onto the couch beside her, still processing. His mind raced through a hundred thoughts -joy, fear, disbelief, responsibility — all tangled together.
Then he reached for her hand and held it firmly.

"How do you feel about it?" he asked gently.

Ayanda exhaled shakily. "Scared. But happy. I didn't plan it, but... I'm happy."

Lebo nodded slowly, emotion thick in his voice."So am I."

They sat together in silence, hands intertwined. Outside, the world carried on - unaware that everything had just changed.

CHAPTER EIGHT
THE DINNER

The days after the news were golden.

Lebo couldn't stop smiling. He would wake before Ayanda just to watch her sleep, his hand resting lightly on her belly that hadn't yet begun to show. They laughed more than they had in months. Every small thing — tea, music, shared glances - felt like a tiny celebration.

He told her one morning, "This baby came at the right time. We needed something to remind us that life is still beautiful."

Ayanda smiled, eyes soft. "So what now?"

He hesitated, then grinned.
 "Now we tell our parents. Properly. And I do this the right way."

They decided to host a dinner - both families together for the first time. It would be at their apartment - small, simple, but full of love.

Ayanda spent the night before the dinner preparing what she was going to cook: she marinated the beef stew, mixed flour for dumplings, marinated the chicken she was going to roast, chopped and diced vegetables. She wanted everything perfect.

Lebo bought flowers, wine, and even borrowed a set of fancy dishes from a colleague. He hadn't told her, but he also bought a ring.

The Arrival

Ayanda's parents arrived first - warm smiles, soft laughter, genuine excitement.
Mama Dlamini hugged Ayanda tightly.

"You're glowing, my girl. This house smells like happiness."

Soon after, Lebo's parents arrived. Mama looked around the apartment with pursed lips.

"So this is where our son's money goes," she murmured to Papa, who only nodded.

The atmosphere was polite - stiff at first, but Ayanda's charm slowly eased it.
Dinner started with laughter. Stories were shared, and even Lebo's father chuckled once or twice. Ayanda's mother kept saying, "Look at these two- young and in love. It's beautiful."

The Proposal

When dessert came, Lebo stood up nervously, cleared his throat, and smiled.
"Before we eat, there's something I want to say."

Ayanda frowned, confused. "Lebo?"

He turned to her, then slowly got down on one knee.

The room went quiet.

"Ayanda Dlamini," he said softly, his voice trembling, "You've been my peace, my light, my home. You've stood by me through everything - through noise, through pressure, through storms.
I can't imagine my life without you. Will you marry me?"

Ayanda gasped, tears instantly flooding her eyes.

"Yes," she whispered, then louder, "Yes!"

The room erupted - her parents clapped, laughing through tears. Even Papa Dlamini stood and hugged Lebo warmly.

But on the other side of the table, Mama and Papa Mokoena sat still.

The Interruption

Finally, Mama Mokoena spoke, her voice calm but sharp.

"I hope this is just a proposal, Lebo."

The joy in the room dimmed slightly.

"Because before there's any wedding" she continued, "you still have to renovate the family house. You know this. We've spoken about it."

Papa Mokoena nodded. "A man must first build his family home before he builds his own and start a family"

Lebo blinked, trying to keep his tone respectful.

"Mama, Papa, we will handle that. But we also want to start our life-"

Mama cut him off. "Oh, of course you do. That's what she wanted all along."

Ayanda's eyes widened. "Excuse me?"

Mama leaned forward slightly. "Don't act innocent, my dear. You've been rushing everything since you met him - moving in, isolating him from his family, now marriage."

Ayanda's mother frowned. "That's uncalled for?'

Mama ignored her. "This is exactly why we warned him. You can't wait because you've already trapped him."

Ayanda's voice trembled. "No, you don't understand—"

"Oh, but I do," Mama said, her tone icy. "You think you can just walk in and-"

Lebo stood suddenly, his voice firm. "No, you don't understand."

The room went silent.

He turned to face his mother directly. "You don't understand because Ayanda is pregnant."

The words hung in the air like thunder.

The Fallout

Everyone froze.
Ayanda's parents gasped — surprised but quickly recovering with warmth.
Her mother stood and hugged her tightly. "Oh, my baby.. congratulations."

Her father looked at Lebo with steady eyes. "Then you must marry her, son. And quickly. Do things right."

But Mama Mokoena was shaking her head, tears forming. "So it's true. You've lost your way."

"Mama, please-"

"No, Lebo. You've brought shame on this family. You can't even afford to finish our house, but now you're having babies?"

Papa Mokoena's voice was low but hard. "We said renovate first. That was our blessing's condition.
And we meant it."

Lebo looked between both sets of parents — two worlds colliding in one room.

Ayanda was crying quietly beside him, and for the first time, he didn't know who to comfort - his mother or the woman carrying his child.

He reached for Ayanda's hand and held it tight.

"If this is wrong," he said quietly, "then I'll spend the rest of my life fixing it."

Mama turned away, muttering under her breath.

"She's already taken everything. Now she'll take him too."

CHAPTER NINE
THE BREAKING POINT

That dinner night ended with broken voices and quiet tears.

Ayanda's mother gently held her hand and said,

"Come home with us tonight, my girl. Let things cool down."

Lebo wanted to protest but saw the exhaustion in Ayanda's eyes - the trembling, the swollen silence.So he simply nodded.

"Okay. Just... text me when you're home."

Her parents guided her out, speaking softly as they left.

Moments later, Lebo's parents also gathered their things.No one said goodbye. The laughter and music that had filled the evening felt like it belonged to another world.

The Next Morning

Sleep had refused to come. Lebo lay awake replaying every word from the night before - the proposal, the joy, the shame. He woke early, showered, dressed neatly, and drove to Ayanda's family home.

When he arrived, Ayanda's father met him at the gate with his usual calm smile.

"Come in, my boy."

Lebo hesitated. "Is she... okay?"

"She's ok," said Mr. Dlamini. "We talked. Come, let's sit."

They sat in the lounge - Ayanda's mother beside her husband, Ayanda sitting quietly with red eyes but composed. Lebo and her eyes met, and they smiled, both looking down shyly.

Mr. Dlamini began,

"We've had time to think. What happened last night was painful, but it doesn't have to destroy anything."

Lebo looked up, surprised.

"We see that you love each other," continued Mr. Dlamini.
"And we trust you. So this is what we've decided - Ayanda will wait. Renovate the house, then you can get married. We know your heart is in the right place. We want you to get your parents' blessings."

Ayanda nodded softly. "We'll do it the right way, babe."

Lebo swallowed hard, emotion filling his throat. He hadn't expected forgiveness.
He stood and shook Mr. Dlamini's hand.

"Thank you, sir. Thank you for believing in me. I won't disappoint you."

New Beginnings

They left together that afternoon, holding hands.Ayanda smiled faintly as they drove home.

"I'm glad my parents understand," she said softly.

Lebo nodded, smiling. "I told you - everything will be fine. I'll start planning the renovations immediately."

For the first time in a long time, he felt hopeful again.He kept his distance from his parents for a while, giving space for tempers to cool.But Ayanda, ever the peacemaker, said one evening,

"Maybe we should go see them, love. Be the bigger people. Just talk. Let them know the plan."

He looked at her for a long moment and smiled.

"You really are something else."

The Visit

That weekend, Ayanda said softly over breakfast,

"Let's go see your parents. Be the bigger people.Let's show them we respect their wishes."

Lebo hesitated, but her eyes carried that same calm faith that had always grounded him.He nodded. "Okay. Let's go."

When they arrived, Mama was hanging laundry in the yard and Papa was trimming the hedge near the tree.They froze for a moment when they saw the car pull in.

Ayanda greeted first, smiling gently. "Good afternoon, Mama. Good afternoon, Papa."

Mama looked away at first, then murmured, "Afternoon, my child."
Papa simply nodded.

Inside, the tension was heavy but polite. Ayanda set down a small cake she'd brought and said,

"We came to talk."

They all sat - Ayanda and Lebo on one couch, his parents opposite.

Lebo started. "We wanted to say we're sorry about how that dinner ended. Things got emotional. But we've decided to wait."

Mama frowned. "Wait?"

Ayanda spoke softly. "Yes, Mama. We'll wait. Lebo will renovate the house first before we plan any wedding. We just want peace, and we respect how you do things."

For a moment, Mama didn't respond. Then, slowly, she nodded.
"That's how we do things indeed," she said, her voice calmer than it had been in months. "I'm glad you finally understand."

Papa gave a small approving smile. "Good. A man must build his family home before he marries.
That's our way."

Lebo exhaled, feeling the tension melt from his shoulders. It was the first time he'd seen both families agree on something - even if it meant postponing his own happiness.

Mama even offered tea. Ayanda accepted it with a smile, and for a fleeting moment, everything felt normal again.

Drowning Quietly

In the weeks that followed, Lebo threw himself into planning the renovations.
Every spare rand went toward materials, contractors, and deposits. He worked overtime, skipped meals, and told Ayanda,

"Just a little longer, babe. Once the house is done, we'll have our wedding."

But the costs piled up faster than his paychecks. Loans, payment plans, promises - they stacked higher and higher until sleep became a stranger.

Ayanda tried to stay positive. She'd rub her growing belly and whisper,

"Daddy's working hard for you."

But she saw the exhaustion in his eyes - the quiet panic he tried to hide with tired smiles.

The Collapse

One Thursday afternoon at work, Ayanda felt dizzy.Her colleagues rushed to her as she held her stomach and whispered,
"Something's wrong."

Her boss drove her straight to the hospital.
By the time Lebo arrived, he found her lying pale and weak on the hospital bed, machines beeping sottly.A nurse touched his shoulder.
"You must be Mr.
Mokoena?"

"Yes," he said breathlessly. "Is she okay? The baby?"

The nurse's face softened. "I'm sorry. She lost the pregnancy."

Lebo froze, his mind refusing to process the words.He walked to her side slowly, his heart pounding.Ayanda looked up at him with glassy eyes.

"I'm sorry," she whispered. "I tried. I really did."

He sat beside her and took her hand, tears spilling silently down his face.He wanted to say it wasn't her fault, that they'd be okay, but no words came out.

They sat there in the dim hospital light, both broken in ways they couldn't name - two people who had tried to do everything right, and still lost everything that mattered most.

CHAPTER TEN
THE GOODBYE

Ayanda's pregnancy was far along - her belly had carried life for months, her dreams already painted in pastel.The loss wasn't small. It wasn't something she could cry about for a week and move on from.It was death - real, heavy, irreversible.

The funeral had to be arranged quickly.
Even as her parents helped with the preparations, there were calls and lists, voices asking,

"Lebo, the workers say they need their pay."
"The renovations must continue."

The irony burned. They were planning a burial while still paying for bricks and paint.
No one paused the house project, not even for grief.

Lebo, numb and exhausted, did what he always did - he paid.He took a loan, telling himself, If I can just finish this house, we can finally start our life.He wanted peace so badly he couldn't see he was bleeding for it.

The Unspoken Distance

Ayanda barely spoke in those days.
She moved through the house like a ghost - cleaning, folding new born baby onesies that wouldn't be worn, sitting quietly by the window.Her heart ached with a sadness words couldn't hold.

She looked at Lebo sometimes and saw the man she loved, but also the man who couldn't stand up for her.The man who had chosen them again - his family, his duties, the unending debt - even after it cost them everything.

When she finally spoke one night, her voice was soft, fragile.

"Babe, I'll handle the funeral arrangements. You sort out your family. They always come first anyway."

Lebo turned to her, guilt flickering in his eyes.

"Ayanda, that's not fair."

She looked at him, tired but calm.

"It's not about fair. It's just the truth."

He took her hands. "You come first, Ayanda. You and I... we'll get through this. I just need to finish the renovations. Once that's done, everything will fall into place."

She smiled faintly, but her heart whispered, That's what you always say.

The Funeral

The day of the funeral was cold and grey.
A small white coffin. A short prayer.The world seemed too quiet to hold that kind of sorrow.

After the burial, everyone returned to Lebo's family home.There was food, murmured condolences, the soft clinking of plates - the strange, polite rituals of mourning.

Ayanda sat between her parents, her body present but her spirit elsewhere. Lebo moved between guests, greeting, thanking, pouring tea - playing host to a grief he hadn't allowed himself to feel.

When the house started to empty, Ayanda's parents stood.

"We'll take Ayanda home," her mother said gently.
"You stay and finish up here. Come later when everyone's gone."

Lebo nodded. "Okay, Mama. I'll come soon."

He kissed Ayanda's forehead. "Rest, babe. I'll see you at home."

She nodded, her eyes distant.

The Decision

In the car, silence filled the space between her and her parents. Then Ayanda spoke quietly.
"I can't do this anymore."

Her mother turned, startled. "Do what, baby?"

"This life. This cycle. After the renovations, it'll be something else. His family. The house. The debt.
I'll never come first."

She stared out the window, tears rolling silently.

"I love him. God knows I do. But I can't forget.Every time I see them, I'll remember why my child isn't here."

Her father sighed deeply. "Are you sure this is what you want?"

"I don't know what I want," she whispered. "But I know I can't heal here. I need to leave - go somewhere far. Maybe another country. Start again."

Her mother's eyes filled with tears. "If that's what you need, my girl, we'll support you."

They drove in silence until they reached her and Lebo's apartment.
Her parents waited in the car while she went inside to pack.

The Letter

The house was quiet, too clean - as if it had already forgotten them.
Ayanda moved slowly, folding clothes, gathering memories that felt heavier than fabric.On the table, she left a note. Her handwriting neat, her heart trembling between every line.

Dear Lebo, my love

You did nothing wrong. Unfortunately, it turned out like this.I know you were trying to please your parents - trying to give us a better life.But our child suffered because of it.The stress from your family weighed too much on me that our child paid the ultimate price.

I don't think I can forget that.It seems you will never be free from this debt you never even owed in the first place.And I can't keep being part of it.

This is goodbye. Don't look for me.By the time you read this, I'll probably be at the airport - or in the sky, heading somewhere I can breathe again.

Until the day you stand up for your family - truly stand up - you will always belong to everyone but yourself.

I love you. Always will.

- Ayanda

She placed the letter where he'd find it easily - right beside the framed ultrasound photo he kept by the couch.

Then she walked out quietly, her parents waiting just outside.

As the door closed behind her, it wasn't just the end of a relationship. It was the end of a woman's patience, the end of her hope - and the beginning of Lebo's awakening.

CHAPTER ELEVEN
THE PRICE OF BEING BORN

When Lebo got home that evening, the silence was heavier than usual. The curtains were half drawn, the air faintly smelled of Ayanda's perfume - that soft jasmine scent that lingered long after she left a room.
He called out once, twice.

"Ayanda?"

No answer.

He passed the kitchen after peeping to see if Ayanda was there then he went straight to their bedroom. The bed was made, the curtains half-drawn, her scent faint but present. He opened the closet — her clothes were gone. In the bathroom, her toothbrush missing and her skincare bottles gone.

He stepped out into the small garden, hoping to find her watering the plants, maybe lost in thought. Nothing. Only the sound of distant cars and the wind brushing the leaves.

Then, back in the living room, he saw it - an envelope on the coffee table, tucked beneath the ultrasound photo. Her handwriting on the front. His heart sank.

He couldn't bring himself to open it yet. Instead, he grabbed his phone and dialed her parents.

Her father answered on the second ring.

"Papa... where is she?" Lebo's voice cracked.

"Son, calm down-"

"She's gone, isn't she?"

A pause.

"Maybe she'll come back," her father said gently. "Give her time."

Lebo's breathing grew shallow. "She's gone," he repeated, almost whispering, then ended the call.

He stood for a long moment, staring at the envelope, then tore it open with shaking hands.

The words hit him like a hammer to the chest. He ran out the door, drove to her parents' house, and when her mother opened the door, he barely managed to speak.

"Mama, please... where is she?"

Her mother's eyes were wet.
"She really left, son. She wasn't coping. She said she needed to start over."

"Where?"

Her mother hesitated.
"Check her email."

Lebo rushed to Ayanda's laptop, opened it, and saw the confirmation immediately.

Flight ticket to Brazil.
Visa-free. Immediate departure. She'd already gone.
He stood there, staring at the screen until the words blurred into nothing.

Flight ticket to Brazil.Departed that afternoon. South Africans didn't need visas. She had gone the moment she could.

His world tilted. He sat down, numb, staring at the glowing screen.

He whispered to himself, "Brazil... she really lefft."

He thanked her parents quietly, walked out, and drove to his parents' house.

The Dismissal

He drove straight to his parents' home, numb. When they saw him walk in, face pale, letter in hand, they froze.

"She left," he said simply, handing them the paper.

Mama took one look and chuckled bitterly.

"Don't worry, she'll be back. She failed to trap you with that baby. Now she's ashamed. Good riddance."

Papa added,

"Focus on work, my boy. A woman who leaves that easily was never a wife."

Lebo didn't speak. He realised there was no point. They'd never understand what they'd done - how their expectations had crushed not just him, but everything he loved.
He walked out quietly, closing the door behind him.

The Breaking Point

Days passed.
He went to work, but his mind wasn't there.
He came home to the silence, the same cold bed, the same empty closet.
He didn't eat much. Didn't talk much. Just existed.

Then one evening, his phone rang.
Ayanda.

He froze before answering.

"Ayanda?"

"Lebo," her voice was steady, distant. "I'm fine. I want you to be okay too. Please move on. As for me... I just need to forget what happened. I'm not coming back."

The line went dead.

He sat for a long time, staring at the phone, her voice echoing in his head.
Then it rang again - his mother.

"My boy, it's month-end. The workers want their money. Don't forget your uncle's taxi fare."

Lebo stared at the wall.

"Fine. I'll send it."

"Good. Before Friday-"

He interrupted.

"In fact, I'll send everything. All the money on me."

"What? Why all of it?"

He didn't answer. He just whispered,

"It's time I paid off my debt."

"What do you mean?"

But he'd already hung up.

He transferred his full salary to them - the entire amount.
The screen flashed: Payment successful.

The Final Payment

After making his final payment he closed his banking app. He poured himself a glass of the red wine he'd bought earlier — then another, then another. The bitterness burned down his throat, but it quieted the ache in his chest.

He opened his notebook - the same one he used to track expenses.
The last page had a neat column titled "Expenses."
He turned the page and began to write his final two notes.

To His Parents

Dear Mama, Papa -
I loved you both so much that I forgot to live.
I tried to repay you for bringing me into the world, not realising I never asked to be here.
You said life was expensive, and I believed you - so I've been paying ever since.
Tonight, I'm making my last payment.
Not only with my last salary but with my life too. No more debt that I never owed.
Please, let my story remind you - love shouldn't be a loan.

-Lebo

He folded it carefully, then reached for another page.

To Ayanda

Dear Ayanda,

You were right - I was never free.
I thought love was giving until there was nothing left. But now I see, real love is freedom - and I never gave us that.

I don't blame you for leaving.
I hope Brazil gives you the peace you never found here.

I'm sorry - to you, to our baby, to myself - for not standing up when it mattered. I will love you always.

- Lebo

He laid the two letters side by side, beside the ultrasound photo.
Then he sat back, tears falling quietly, a faint smile breaking through the pain.

The glass trembled slightly as he poured the last of the wine, watching the deep red swirl and settle.

On the table, an open bottle of pills lay beside two folded notes and an ultrasound photo- untouched but waiting.

He sat back, staring at the ceiling, his breathing steady, almost calm.

For the first time in a long while, the silence didn't frighten him.

The clock ticked once. Then again.
He lifted the glass slowly, his eyes soft - as if finally at peace.

Aftermath - "The Morning After"

It was his landlord who noticed first.
The lights had been on all night, and the car still parked in the same spot.
He knocked. No answer.
He called. The phone rang from inside the apartment.

A strange, heavy stillness filled the hallway.
When the door was finally opened by the building manager, the room was quiet — too quiet.
The curtains moved gently in the morning breeze.
On the table sat the two letters, neatly folded beside a half-empty glass and a framed photo of Ayanda's ultrasound.

The police came. Then his parents. Then silence again.

Word spread quickly - Lebo is gone.

Nobody had the courage to ask how. They didn't need to. The notes said everything.

Reactions

Mama collapsed when she saw his handwriting.
Papa sat on the floor and just stared at the photo, whispering,

"He paid. My boy really thought he owed us."

Ayanda got the call in Brazil. She sat on her hotel bed for hours, staring out at the ocean she had hoped would bring her peace.
Her hands trembled as she opened the message from Lebo's cousin. There was a photo of the two letters - his last words.

Tears blurred her vision. She whispered to the wind,

"Lebo, I'm so sorry. I never wanted this. I just wanted you to live for you."

She pressed her hand against her chest as if she could somehow reach across the distance and stop time.
But it was too late.

The Legacy

At the funeral, people spoke of Lebo as the good son - the dependable one, the quiet one, the one who "always gave."
But in Ayanda's eulogy, her voice trembling but clear, she said:

"Lebo didn't die because he was weak. He died because love without balance becomes a burden.

He gave until he disappeared, because no one taught him that love doesn't mean debt."

The room was silent - the kind of silence that humbles even pride.
Even his parents couldn't look up.

And from that day on, his story travelled quietly through homes and families, carried by whispers, sermons, and school talks - a reminder that children are not born to repay their parents, but to live their own lives.

Author's Reflection - For Every Child Who Thinks They Owe Their Parents Their Life

This story isn't just about Lebo
It's about every son and daughter who grew up believing that love must always be repaid.

We are taught that gratitude means sacrifice, that "good children" give until it hurts.
But love was never meant to be a transaction.
It was meant to be a home.

Lebo's story is a mirror held up to many - the firstborns, the dependables, the quiet providers who mistake exhaustion for duty and guilt for love. It's also a call to parents: to love without turning that love into lifelong debt.

No child owes a parent for being born.
Birth is a gift, not a loan.

Parents raise children so they can rise - not so they can repay.
And children should give from abundance, not from fear.

If you are reading this and you recognise yourself in Lebo - if you feel buried under expectation, guilt or obligation - please remember:
you are allowed to breathe.
you are allowed to say no.
you are allowed to live.

Let The Price of Being Born remind you that love cannot be measured by money, loyalty is not slavery, and that peace sometimes begins the moment you stop paying for your own existence.

ABOUT THE AUTHOR

Thuli Marutle Leigh is a South African-born author and international ESL teacher whose work reflects the complexities of family, sacrifice, and identity. Drawing from real-life experiences, she brings to light the emotional and cultural weight of expectations that often follow one's birthright.

In The Price of Being Born, Thuli explores the unspoken burden of "black tax" - the sense of obligation carried by many who strive to uplift their families while building lives of their own. Through honest storytelling and heartfelt reflection, she gives voice to a truth that many live but few are willing to confront.

www.ingramcontent.com/pod-product-compliance
Lightning Source LLC
Chambersburg PA
CBHW032058150426
43194CB00006B/571